RICHES
and
FACETS
LYON of

Text and Photographs
Gérald GAMBIER

EDITIONS
LA TAILLANDERIE

COLLECTION
RICHES AND FACETS
Directed by Gérald Gambier

Infography : Patricia Brun
English translation : Hedwige West

© Editions La Taillanderie - 2006
rue des Frères-Lumière
01400 Châtillon-sur-Chalaronne
Tél : 04 74 55 16 59
e-mail : editions-la-taillanderie@cegetel.net
www.la-taillanderie.com

ISBN 2-87629-344-7
ISSN pending

CONTENTS

Bank of the enchanting Saône.

Rue Juiverie, on the hôtel Dugas, the city's emblem.

Historical Chronology

5ᵗʰ Century BC: Gaulois housing in Gorge-de-Loup

58 BC: Julius Cesar camps on the heights of Fourvière

43 BC (October 9): Munatius Plancus founds the roman colony known as Lugdunum on Fourvière.

27 BC: Augustus makes Lugdunum the capital of Gaul, and introduces the cult of the imperial person.

19 BC: Agrippa sets out the first four main roads out of Lugdunum.

16 BC: Augustus has a 4000-seat theatre built in Fourvière.

12 BC: Drusus inaugurates the federal sanctuary where the 60 Gaulois tribes will meet.

Construction of the first two aqueducts started.

10 BC: Birth of the emperor Claudius in Lugdunum.

19 AD: construction of the Trois Gaules theatre near the sanctuary on the Croix-Rousse.

48 AD: Emperor Claudius obtains from the Senate that Lyonnais people can become citizens of Rome. Construction of the Brévenne aqueduct.

65 AD: Lugdunum fire. Emperor Neron offers the town four million sesterces in compensation.

117 to 138: Hadrien reigns. The Croix-Rousse amphitheatre is rebuilt to accommodate

Lyon, Laughter and Tears

For the first time visitor to Lyon, it is the *Fourvière* mount, with its basilica for an acropolis, which seems to symbolise the city. As it happens, the basilica itself (and not the steel tower, which is not open to the public) is a perfect spot to take in a 360-degree view of the town. It is only later, as one reaches the *place Bellecour* that the topography of the site becomes clear. Two rivers, one the largest of its kind in France, and three mounts: the praying mount of Fourvière, the working mount of *la Croix-Rousse*, and *la Duchère*.

The *Rhône* river is strong and majestic but not half as wild as it used to be since works were carried

20,000 people. In Fourvière the ampitheatre becomes a 10,000 seater. Construction of the Gier aqueduct. Construction of the games arena.

150: birth of the church in Lyon at Saint-Nizier.

160: Construction of the Fourvière Odeon and of the Cybèle temple finished.

177: First local Christian martyrs: Blandine, Pothin and 47 others are tortured and killed.

197: Emperor Septime Sévère defeats Albinus who comes to hide in Lugdunum. The town is pillaged.

Fourth century: the barbarians attack the Roman Empire. Because raids have robbed the town of the lead lining of the aqueduct, the town runs out of water. The population settles on the banks of the Saône.

457: the Burgondes troops occupy Lugdunum and rename the town Lugdon.

Early Middle Ages.

549: Saint Sacerdos is the bishop asked by king Childebert (son of Clovis) and Queen Ultrogoth to build the first hospital, ancestor of the Hôtel-Dieu. The Orléans Council declares its promise of protection and independence.

798-814: Leidrade, first archbishop of Lyon, invested by Charlemagne, gives the Lyon church a new lease of life.

840: the Trajan forum collapsed.

843: at the Verdun treaty, Lyon is given to Lothaire.

879: Lyon becomes the capital of the Provence Realm. At its head is Boson, Charles le Chauve's brother in law.

935: Hungarians come and plunder the town. The Ainay Abbey is in ruins.

The Middle Ages

1032 : integration of Lyon to the Holy Germanic Empire.

1050 to1071: construction of the stone bridge, also called Pont du Change, across the Saône.

out to raise its banks, thus gaining more land where the two rivers converge at *Perrache*.

These waters have long been the scene of jousting competitions: opposing teams of local lifeguards use wooden poles to tip their opponents into the waters. This tradition has survived to the present day and two or three contests can be seen every year, either in Lyon, or at *la Mulatière*.

The *Saône* is a calm and lazy river. The Romans named it Arar and Julius Cesar threw his coat in the water near Trevoux, in order to make out which way it flowed. The Saône acts as a muse for poets and photographers and that may be why all the second-hand book dealers of Lyon chose its left bank to set up shop.

The *presqu'île* (peninsula) is thus bordered by both rivers, and indeed the people of Lyon think of it as an island. Since the presqu'île is always approached from the same side, the Lyonnais people will refer to the Saône side as the Right Bank and the Rhône as the Left Bank.

Fourvière is the birthplace of the city and of its faith, and is still today the guardian of its piety. Only a few joyous church festivals break up the grave religious fervour of the area: the Gregorian Lætare chants at Easter, the Gaudete at Christmas, and, on the eighth of December, an exuberant celebration of the town's delivery from the Plague in 1643 which has been remembered ever since - see page 74.

On the Croix-Rousse, people seem much more down to earth. The name dates from the nineteenth century when silk weaving was the main business in the city, with workers enduring punishing shifts for pitiful pay.

Au bouchon La Mère Cottivet, rue Palais-Grillet, a very typical bouliste decor.

Since the middle ages Lyon has left its mark on the world silk trade. Silk, that exotic fibre, is subject to today's exaggerated labour costs compared with those of other countries. The local trade is boosted by the demands of tourism and Haute Couture, but the production is still relatively modest. Modern textile industries still benefit in many ways from Croix-Rousse skills and weaving techniques. This means that Lyon is still regarded as an authority by the international silk manufacturing industry.

The trade endures also in the *Musée des Tissus* (Museum of Textiles) situated within the eighteenth century Hotel de Villeroy. Here one can travel through 2,000 years of weaving and interior decoration, illustrated by fabrics from the four corners of the world, with particular emphasis on the local pro-

A wide-ranging view from Fourvière.

1079 : the archbishop of Lyon receives the title of 'Primat des Gaules'.

1084 : construction of the current Saint Paul church starts.

1107 : consecration of the new Ainay abbey by Pope Pascal II.

1157 : In a new law named the 'Bulle d'Or', Frédéric Barberousse confirms the temporal authority of the archbishop on the city.

1165 : construction of the Saint-Jean-Baptiste cathedral under way.

1180 : a wooden bridge is erected across the Rhône. Edification of the first chapel dedicated to the Virgin Mary and to Saint Thomas Becket, in Fourvière.

1245 : first council of Lyon, called by Pope Innocent IV, to decide on the excommunication of Frédéric II Barberousse.

1268 : the bourgeois citizens of the city rise against the archbishop's rule.

1274 : second council of Lyon, called by Pope Gregory X, which ratifies the brief reunification of the Churches of the Orient and the Occident.

1305 : rather timid start of the erection of the church in Saint-Nizier. Pope Clement V is crowned in the collegiate church in Saint-Just.

1316 : election of Pope John XXII at the Jacobin convent.

1320 : Lyon is joined to the French crown. Birth of Lyon as a regional administrative centre.

1326 : construction of Saint-Bonaventure church.

1348-1363 : endemic spread of the black plague.

1420 : Charles VII founds the first three fares in Lyon.

1436 : first 'Rebeyne' – rebellion of the lower classes.

Renaissance

1460 : the Medici family transfer their bank from Geneva to Lyon.

1463 (March 8 th) : edict from the king Louis XI allowing Lyon to hold four fares a year.

duction. Through the quality of its exhibitions, its exhaustive documentation centre (holding over 30,000 works), its textile picture library, its restoration centre and its International Centre for the Study of Old Textiles, the Musée des Tissus has become an international centre for creative textile manufacture. And indeed it has also become the home of the Association Internationale de la Soie.

The *Musée des Arts Decoratifs* compliments the Musée des Tissus, illustrating the use of textiles and tapestries in seventeenth and eighteenth century interior design.

It was among the workers of the Croix-Rousse and the presqu'île, and those of *Montchat* and Vaulx-en-Velin, where most Italian immigrants settled, that the famous game of *Boule Lyonnaise* became established. It is known to its devotees as *la longue* (the long one). Sadly the tradition is dying out, and few bistros nowadays still own a longue pitch. However it is still a popular sport in the town, mostly in squares and on the banks.

In describing Lyon, one has to examine the character of the city's typical inhabitants and their taste for secrecy and discretion. Felix Benoit defined Lyon as '*a town where one laughs, as one makes love, in private*'.

Even though the city is now a major player on an international scale, two thousand years of local tradition has forged a middle class for whom the saying '*pour vivre heureux, vivons cachés*' (to live happy is to live hidden) still stands. Publications such as *Monsieur Lyon* and *Lyon Mag* demonstrate that the local atmosphere has changed little from that of the fifties, when Henri Beraud wrote *Ciel de Suie*.

Illuminated sculptures on the Pont de Lafayette (1818), crossing le Rhône. Under the pont Lafayette, narrow boats and the hôtel-Dieu.

1473: Bartholomew Buyer calls the Belgian typographer Guillaume Le Roy to whom the first book to be published in the city is due. On May 17th 1473, the Compendium of Pope Innocent III comes off the presses. By the sixteenth century, Lyon Printers are the most famous in the world.

1527: foundation of the Trinity College by Jesuit monks.

1528: discovery of half of Claudius's table in a Croix-Rousse vineyard.

1529: second 'rebeyne', this time against wheat taxes.

1531: creation of a temporary almsgiving set-up from the city to fight famine amongst its population. It will become the 'Aumône Générale' (general alms) in 1534.

1532-1535: Rabelais is a doctor in the Hôtel-Dieu. He publishes Pantagruel then Gargantua in Lyon.

1536: Etienne Turquet and Barthélemy Nariz install the first silk-weaving looms in the Saint-Georges area of town. Construction of the Hôtel Bullioud and its original galery by Philibert de l'Orme.

1540: By special royal dispensation from François 1er, Lyon becomes the only silk depository in the whole of France.

1555: the cultured salons of the fashionable poet Louise Labé open their doors.

1560: erection of the first mission cross made of golden stone from Couzon, which gave its name to the the Croix-Rousse (red cross). Completion of the stone bridge on the Rhône.

1562 (April): The huguenots of the baron of Adrets invade Lyon. Pillage, destruction and rape come one after another until June 1563. The people of Lyon are to get their revenge during the Lyonnaise St Bartholomew massacre.

1598: edict of Nantes.

1600: at the St John the Baptist cathedral, marriage of king Henri IV and Marie de Medici.

Seventeenth century

1605: setting up of a new type of loom by Claude Dangon, which allows the canuts (weavers) to weave in patterns.

Lyon has long suffered from being notoriously supplanted by *Paris* as the capital of the France. It was a close run contest: when the Dauphin died in Lyon in the early sixteenth century, the king his father, Francois 1er, reversed his decision to make it the country's capital. Hopes were raised yet again, only to be consequently dashed, when Napoleon proclaimed, overwhelmed by the triumphant welcome the city gave him, '*Lyonnais, je vous aime*' (People of Lyon I love you).

It is now an accepted fact that Lyon will shine and be recognised for many special features, but will never be the capital of France.

During the French Revolution at the end of the eighteenth century, Lyonnais people became considered reactionary, when they were actually simply exercising their desire for independence and their customary reticence to be told what to do. In the nineteen forties, De Gaulle, in one well-known speech, even declared the city '*capitale de la Resistance*'. It is true that the region's underground organisations formed a crucial part of the French Resistance. Nowadays, the *Centre d'Histoire de la Resistance et de la Deportation* keeps the flame burning. It is housed in the old military health school which was the headquarters of the Gestapo under the Occupation. It is a very well conceived exhibition with a remarkably objective outlook, where the visitor is led step by step through the events of the World War II. The walls and the use of darkness evoke a powerful sense of oppression and imprisonment.

Paradoxically, Lyon is most reserved about those aspects of its life in which it should take most

The elegant bridge leading across the Saône to the Court House (1984, Lamboley-Delfante).

Second-hand bookdealers on the bank of the Saône.

A view of the Saône from the Vaise fort.

1607 : the construction of the Trinity College and of its chapel (currently the Ampère high school) is under way.

1617 : start of the edification of the Hospice de la Charité thanks to the Aumône Générale.

1622 to 1631: extension of the Hospital-du-Pont-du-Rhône, later called Hôtel-Dieu.

1643 (September 8 th): the city's aldermen vow their faith to the Virgin Mary and the city is blessed to try to protect it from further plague epidemics. The town is never again touched by the disease.

1646 : start of the construction of the new Hôtel de Ville for the man responsible for the construction and upkeep of the city's roads and bridges: Simon Maupin.

1659 : start of the construction Saint-Pierre convent (now the Musée des Beaux-Arts).

1667 : Colbert regulates the Grande Fabrique Lyonnaise de la soierie (silk works).

1700 : J. Hardouin-Mansart rebuilds the town hall, which had burned down in 1674.

Eighteenth century

1713 : statue of Louis XIV in Bellecour, by sculptor Tony Desjardins.

1730 : construction of the Hôtel de Villeroy (Musée des Tissus).

1733 : Saint-Bruno church is completed.

1744 : first strike of the silk workers against the new Vaucanson weaving loom.

1739-1764: works in Germain Soufflot: extension of the Hôtel-Dieu and its façade on the Rhône, building of the Loge du Change in the old part of town as well as the Grand Théâtre. Urbanisation of the Saint-Clair area.

1761 : Bourgelat founds the first veterinary school in the world.

1764 : Morand urbanises the left bank of the Rhône and starts a wooden bridge to link the town with Brotteaux.

1773 : In Perrache works start to gain some land on the confluent of the Rhône and Saône at La Mulatière.

pride. The Lyonnais remain surprisingly modest about their skill and eminence in the manufacture of jewellery. Can one attribute this to a certain bourgeois reluctance to discuss or indeed expose one's wealth?

Traditionally, the city's fame lies in its gastronomy, and Lyon has been making the most of its reputation in this domain. In 1934, the famous Maurice Edmond Saillard, the precursor of our present day *Michelin restaurant Guide*, proclaimed the town '*the capital of good food*'. He was only confirming the cult of good fare which is deeply rooted in the area's traditions. Saillard went by the name of Curnonsky, which was a name he had made up, at a time when all things Russian were very fashionable, by thinking of the Russian-sounding ending sky, and then using the latin version of the phrase: why-not- sky.

It is not surprising then that the ambassador of French cuisine should be Paul Bocuse, born and bred in Lyon. It is in Lyon as well that the prestigious culinary competition he created still takes place every year.

The city's architectural heritage has also met with particular success. Since the nineteen fifties, a crusade led by a local pressure group for the protection and restoration of the old town has persuaded the local government to renovate and embellish the city's buildings. This effort has paid dividends in terms of tourism. Local politicians have used their international weight to put through a successful application at Unesco for Lyon to form part of the World Heritage List.

Spectacular interiors from the Museums of Textile and the Arts Décoratifs.

The Historical museum of Lyon, also called 'Gadagne', is changing its appearance until 2003. It tells the story of the town, from the Middle Ages to the twenty first century with exhibits covering archaeology, china, furniture, pewter, art, etc. One of its sections constitutes the international museum of puppetry.

1783 (July 15 th) : Claude de Jouffroy d'Abbans rides his steamboat up the Saône, calling it a 'pyroscaphe'.

1784 : ascension of the first hot air balloon at Brotteaux.

1786 : canut strikes to obtain better salaries.

1789 : in July, riots destroy the city's tollgates.

1792 : Chalier imposes a 'sans-culotte' dictatorship. He is guillotined the following year.

1793 (August-October) : siege of Lyon by the troops of the revolutionary Convention.

1793 (12 October) : a Convention decree states : 'Lyon n'est plus' (Lyon is no more).

1800 : Bonaparte rides through Lyon after the battle of Marengo.

Nineteenth century

1804: Pope Pie VII stays in Lyon on his way to Napoléon's coronation.

1806 : Jacquard invents the mechanical loom.

1808 : Laurent Mourguet creates a puppet he names Guignol.

1814 : Napoléon is back from exile on Elbe island and is welcomed triumphantly by the citizens of Lyon. Overwhelmed, he declares : 'Lyonnais, je vous aime'.

1825 : second statue of Louis XIV in Bellecour by Lemot.

1827 : architects Pollet and Chenavard transform the opera.

1831 and 1834 : canut rebellion. Their slogan 'vivre en travaillant ou mourir en combattant' (we'll earn a living or fight to the death).

1832 : Marc Seguin links Lyon to Saint-Etienne by train in six hours.

1834 : the town is protected from all sides by fortifications.

1834-1870: cardinal Bonald brings about a renewal in the catholic faith.

1835 : Baltard starts the construction of the Palais de Justice (Law Court).

1840 : the highest rise of the level of the waters of the Saône ever to be recorded.

Musée de la Résistance : reconstitution of a small town square on the heights of the Croix-Rousse.

Deriving from an old Fourvière tradition, the *Plan Lumière* (Illuminations Project) is now well known to tourists. The city's night-scape is enriched by 270 illuminated sites every night.

The city's artistic renown could and should be enhanced by its numerous murals. There are more than 150 painted walls throughout the city, but their presence seems neither to have been recognised nor exploited. In 2000 alone, two important murals have disappeared under new rendering. Since some of those works have already been recognised by Unesco, it seems wayward for the city not to value these distinguished modern frescoes and preserve them for future generations.

Since 1980, Lyon has played an important part in the world of contemporary dance, with such projects as the now biannual dance festival and Guy Darmet's *Maison de la Danse*. The Conservatoire

National de Musique de Lyon has now included dance in its curriculum. The Dance School is housed in the old Veterinary School and the eighteenth century convent of St Elisabeth on the Quai Chauveau. It also uses rooms in the Grenier d'Abondance (the old cereal store) situated on the opposite bank. In this historical environment, 500 musicians and 50 dancers, about 15 % of whom come from abroad, prepare various national diplomas. Numerous shows are organised throughout the year, many of which are free to the public.

Next to the Grenier d'Abondance is another centre for local art called the Subsistances. It is the most recent of the city's great rehabilitated buildings, set in the old St Marie des Chaînes convent, which the military had been using since 1807. This example of a city's support for its local artistic creation is rather unusual. Les Subsistances is a space devoted to the creation and distribution of artistic projects of crucial originality, daring and relevance. It is an open laboratory for all aspects of contemporary art.

What about cinema, creative writing, publishing, one might ask. Here perhaps Lyon may be said to have lacked intuition and foresight, in the same way that the inventors of cinema themselves, the Lumière brothers, came to doubt the future of their own invention.

To possess such a resource and not exploit it for almost 100 years could be labelled shameful neglect. These days the reputation of Cannes and Courchevel as centres of cinema seems unshakeable. The centenary celebrations of cinema might well have furnished the opportunity for a great project in Lyon, but they went by virtually unnoticed – a single mural

Conservatoire national supérieur de musique et de danse: the Chabrol amphitheatre where doctor Bourgelat used to dissect animals.

1852 : an imperial decree divides the city in 5 administrative areas and adds the areas of Croix-Rousse, Vaise, Montchat and Guillotière.

1852 (December 8th) : first illuminations.

1856 : construction of the Tête D'Or Park by the Bülher brothers.

1857 : Perrache railway station is opened.

1860 : construction of the Palais du Commerce and creation of the rue Impériale (rue de la République) through Vaïsse.

1863 : foundation of the Crédit Lyonnais Bank.

1868 : création of the local newspaper 'Le Progrès'.

1872: construction starts on the Fourvière basilica.

1876 : construction starts on the university on the Claude Bernard embankment.

1877 : théâtre des Célestins.

1879 : creation of the Omnibus and Tramways company.

1884 : count Hilaire de Chardonnet invents artificial silk.

1890 : construction by Pollet of the 'Hôtel de la Préfecture et du Conseil Général' ends.

1892 : installation of the Bartholdi fountain, place des Terreaux.

1895 : the Lumière brothers invent the 'cinématographe'.

Twentieth century

1901 : Marius Berliet opens a factory in Montplaisir.

1904 : start of the construction of the Brotteaux station.

1905 : Edouard Herriot is elected mayor of Lyon. He is to remain in post for 52 years.

1909 : start of the construction of the abattoirs and of the cattle market in Gerland by Tony Garnier.

1910 : The city's main streets are lit up with electricity.

1913-1930: construction of the Hôpital Edouard Herriot in Grange-Blanche by Tony Garnier.

In the Printing Museum, founded in 1964 by Maurice Audin in the fifteenth century hôtel de la Couronne, a lyonnais hand-press built from fifteenth century plans.

Institut Lumière : the first ever décor of the history of cinema. The warehouse where the first film was shot in 1895 has been preserved.

near the *Cour Gambetta* commemorates the event. Happily, this glorious heritage is not altogether lost ; the *Institut Lumière* situated since 1982 in the *Château Lumière* is a museum cum film library, which aims to preserve cinematic heritage through books, films and posters but also exhibitions, training and the showing of old films.

The situation is being greatly improved by the activities of a Croix Rousse based company : *Rhône-Alpes Cinema*. Using a system of advance payments to enable film makers to finance the making, promotion and distribution of their work.

Thanks to their help, over 90 films have been shot in the region, among them *Le Hussard sur le*

Château Lumière : the Lumière brothers' winter garden.

1913 : construction of the Gerland stadium by Tony Garnier.

1916 : the 'foires de Lyon' (annual fares) are reinstated.

1922 : opening of the Rhodiaceta à Vaise and Bron airport.

1925 : start of the construction of the Cité des Etats-Unis by Tony Garnier.

1926 : start of the construction of the Bourse du Travail by Charles Meysson.

1930 : the Fourvière mount caves in on the13th of November.

1931 : construction starts on the skyscrapers in Villeurbanne.

1934 : demolition of the Hospice de la Charité; the steeple alone remains thanks to popular pressure.

1935 : start of the construction of the Hôtel des Postes.

1942 (November): the German army occupies the city.

1943 (May 15th): Jean Moulin founds the Conseil National de la Résistance. On June 21 st, he is arrested by the Gestapo.

1943 : Antoine de Saint-Exupéry writes 'Le Petit Prince'.

1944 : American planes bomb Vaise and Guillotière. The Germans blow up all the bridges except that of l'Homme de la Roche.

1950 : creation of the society for the preservation of the old town, 'Renaissance du Vieux-Lyon'.

1952 : opening of the Croix-Rousse tunnel.

1957 : Louis Pradel is elected mayor.

1958 : construction of the Duchère area and of the Doua campus.

1964 : the old part of town (Vieux-Lyon) is the first listed area of France thanks to the 'loi Malraux'.

1965 : start of the construction of the Tonkin area in Villeurbanne. The flea market is moved to Feyssine.

1967 : construction of the Part-Dieu area is under way.

1968 : création of COURLY (COmmunauté URbaine de LYon) which unites 56 communes.

In the old Pasteur Institute buildings, the Marcel Mérieux laboratories, the P4 Jean Mérieux centre and the European centre for Immunology and Virology.

toit, Les Enfants du Marais, un crime au paradis, and *Lucie Aubrac.*

In 2000, first local commercial film studios opened in Villeurbanne. Perhaps Lyon is finally assuming the Hollywood-style image that it has deserved for more than a century.

In the realm of printing and publishing, successive Lyon governments seem to have ignored all opportunities. Historically, Lyon has been a leader in the field; Rabelais and Nostradamus used to look to Lyon for the publication of their writing. Nowadays, the city is no longer equipped for the work and authors go to Paris or elsewhere. The current administration seems to have been deaf to calls for change and has failed to support the local industry.

Given this situation, the excellent Imprimerie Museum alone is left to present the history of printing and its techniques through the ages, particularly of the Lyon trade and its golden age in the seventeenth century. It also offers specialised training to initiate children and adults alike in various printing techniques.

Lyon has more recently been recognised for its importance to the world of biology. The number of laboratories in the *Gerland* area alone testify to this recognition. The European Centre for Virology has also made the city its home, and so has the P4, the world watchdog for transmissible diseases, which deals with viruses such as Ebola or Lassa.

Several educational facilities were recently set up in the vicinity of the new leisure park in the Gerland area, emphasising the area's dedication to scientific research. the ENS (National School for Science) was established behind the *Tony Garnier* Market.

Opposite page: brought into service in 1964, the refinery of Feyzin contributes to the dynamism of the Rhone-Alps area.

Then its Literary and Humanities equivalents were relocated there from St Cloud and an extension of the University of Lyon I was recently built on the same campus. A new programme aptly called le *boulevard scientifique* is planned, to promote cooperation between researchers, producers and training structures.

Another great local success is a business called *Infograme Entertainment*. This is a start-up company created in 1983 dealing in Computer games and interactive technologies. It is the European leader in its field and its head offices in *Vaise* are an exceptional example of modern architecture.

Plans are afoot to build a Science Museum at the confluent of the Rhône and the Saône.

In 2001, blue and white *Citadis* tramways arrived on the streets, at the same time as the metro was extending towards Gerland. The new *Cristallis* trolley buses also appeared at that time. This however has not solved all parking and traffic problems. The city authorities have finally recognised the deficiencies of local arrangements and a western circular road is planned to avoid traffic congestion in the city centre.

In June 2000, the Lyon *Satolas* airport was renamed in honour of *Antoine de Saint-Exupéry*, born in Lyon in 1900 and lately voted best writer of the 20th century.

In the northern part of town, the second half of the *Cité Internationale* has recently been launched, under the direction of architect Renzo Piano who conceived the first buildings. It comprises a hall seating 3000 and offering 4,000 square meters of new exhibition space, as well as an

In the shape of four boats, the buildings housing the headquarters of Infogrames Entertainment evokes the fluvial past of the area. Creation by Sud Architectes Lyon.

Opposite page : the Grenier d'Abondance with the royal arms on its frontispiece.

1998 (December 5th): the historical site of Lyon is listed in the World Heritage List by Unesco.

1999: ten years of the Plan Lumière. First Festival de la Lumière.

2000: the casino opens in the Cité Internationale.

2001 (January): first tram line opens.

2001 (February): inauguration of the headquaters of Infograme in Vaise.

2001 (March): Gérard Collomb élu maire.

2001: in football, the Lyon football club O.L. wins the League Cup.

2001 (May 19th): a new national stamp commemorates the old part of town.

2002-2006: the Lyon football club O.L. wins championships of France.

Lyon in figures

population: 445 274 inhabitants (Rec. 1999)
area: 4 575 ha (rivers not counted)
Area listed by Unesco: 476 ha
Latitude: 45°43'23"nord
Longitude: 4°56'37"est
Altitude: town centre: 170 m
       Croix-Rousse: 250 m
       Fourvière: 300 m
9 administrative areas
29 bridges (railway bridges included)
Rate of flow of theRhône (as it comes into Lyon):
600 square meters per seconds
Rate of flow of theRhône (after the confluent):
1020 square meters per seconds
59 churches
252 620 jobs
42 métro stations
29,3 km of metro railway
440 000 users per day
39 tram stations
18,6 km tram railway in 2001
Town budget in 2001: 3,603 millions of Francs
(549 millions of Euros)

Le Grand Lyon:

area 49 346 ha
55 administrative areas
2 517 km of roads
Villeurbanne: 127 299 habitants.

international conference centre. It also houses the first Casino ever permitted in an inland city with no spa – a jackpot indeed!

For its future, Lyon also looks towards the south, with the Gerland development, the relocation of the wholesale market to *Corbas* on the south presqu'île beyond Perrache and a planned restructuring of the whole area.

As the 21st century starts, Lyon has all the means to realise its ambitions. The city's two most recent administrations have shown that, given the right conditions and with the good will of the population, the city and the region are capable of great things. Lyon, situated at the very heart of Europe, is poised to face its third millennium.

The tramways are back in town since January 2nd 2001.

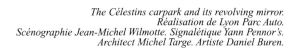

The Célestins carpark and its revolving mirror.
Réalisation de Lyon Parc Auto.
Scénographie Jean-Michel Wilmotte. Signalétique Yann Pennor's.
Architect Michel Targe. Artiste Daniel Buren.

Opposite page: the grandiose wing-shaped entrance of the TGV station at the Lyon Saint-Exupéry airport. Architect: Calatrava

Rue Saint-Jean, the heart
of the old town, which
prompted the application
to Unesco.

Lyon, World Heritage City

December 5th 1998 is a particularly special day in the history of Lyon. On that day, Lyon's entire historic site was officially accepted as part of the World Heritage by the Unesco Committee gathered in Kyoto, Japan.

The adventure started in 1995, when Regis Neyret, previously the president of the *Renaissance du Vieux-Lyon association* whose aim was to preserve the old town, launched the idea that an application should be put forward for the old parts of town to be added to the Unesco's World Heritage List.

Since 1972, the Unesco had looked to identify and protect natural or cultural sites which presented exceptional universal value for future generations.

A delegate from Unesco, M. Azzedine Beschaouch, was invited by the Renaissance du Vieux Lyon association to work out which parts of town were most likely to be accepted. The application thus included the medieval and renaissance parts of the city, as wel as the Gallo-roman site of Lugdunum which marks an essential historical period for Lyon. But the commission which studied the application did not stop there, a much wider area was selected than the one put forward originally: it incorporated the eighteen century fortifications as well.

So now, more than 10 % of the city itself are inclu-ded in the historical site, four hundred and seventy seven hectares to be exact, stretching from the Old Lyon centre to *Fourvière*, *Saint-Just*, *Croix-Rousse* and three quarters of the *Presqu'île* peninsula.

In the Hôtel Bullioud, a gallery created in 1536 by Lyon's own Philibert de l'Orme, when he was only 26 years old.

The fact that Lyon's past can be read in its buildings extends to its important growth in the nineteenth century. This building was a 'Café-concert', then a theatre in 1877 before it became the home of the city's newspaper 'Le Progrès'. The edifice was rebuilt by architect Prosper Perrin in 1894, keeping its facade.

What is noticeable is that those areas correspond to areas where people actually live, they are not at all set in some kind of museum. One can read in those buildings the successive steps the city went through before becoming what it is now: the result of the meticulous work of a hundred generations of Lyonnais.

This echoes particularly well the attitude that Unesco took when it described the city as *'a magnificent example of human settlement, which represents an exceptional testimony of the continuity of two millennia of urban community'*.

The World Heritage List comprises six hundred sites and monuments, twenty two of which are French: Saint-Michael's Mount, the Saint-Madeleine basilica in Vézelay, the Piana seaside calanques, the Gard bridge as well as the castle of Versailles. French towns are not very often listed, Lyon shares the stage with the petite France in Strasbourg, Avignon and the medieval town in Carcassonne.

Lyon is in fact the next biggest urban city on the list after Prague, sitting pretty among Venice, Saint Petersburg, Salzburg, Naples, Cordoba, Toledo, and Quebec.

At the end of a fifty year long battle for the preservation of the city's historical buildings and about ten years of restoration, Lyon is now starting to receive the recognition it deserves. It has now proved how far it has come since Baudelaire called it *ville de charbon* (city of coal).

Exit *Myrlingues* fog and *Ciel de suie* (sooty skies)! Now people can but acknowledge the fact that the ugly duckling has become a swan. Lyon is a bright city, full of life and colour, indeed one of the most beautiful in the world.

The Chapelle de la Trinité, in the Lycée Ampère, a restored legacy from the baroque past of the city.

The pink tower, one of the symbols of the Renaissance in Lyon which is so striking to visitors.

Lyon, gallo-roman town

The first human settlement on the site of the town seems to date from the end of the paleolithic (ten thousand to six thousand BC), near the *Duchère plateau*. At that time, man stayed away from the *Rhône* and the *Saône*. The rivers' courses were not set and they flooded very often.

From the neolithic (six thousand to two thousand BC), the settlement shifts to the bank of the

Detail from a tomb in place Eugène Wernert. In 1885, archaeologists carried out digs in Trion and discovered a row of monumental tombs along the roadside of the Voie d'Aquitaine, dating from the first century.

Rhône, from Saint-Priest to Anse. Later, the Bronze Age and then the Iron Age man's community spread to the Duchère hills and the *Vaise* plains. Curiously, it is even before its conquest of the Gaul that Rome influences the local life, mainly with money and potery from as early as 140 BC. In 58 BC, as he sets off on his Gallic Wars, Julius Caesar sets up his first camp on Fourvière. *Lugdunum* was the second town of the Roman Empire, but unfortunately, written accounts of its foundation are extremely rare. It is thus essentially through archeology and epigraphy that the controversial points of the early life of the city can be made out.

If Cicero's writings are to be taken for granted, in 44 BC, a rebellion of the inhabitants of Vienna against the Roman veterans of the 5th Legion explains why they were expelled from Vienna. Those soldiers had been positioned in Vienna by Caesar who wanted to keep an eye on the rather hostilecolony, but after his assassination, in March 44 BC, the local political unrest forced the soldiers to move on and they ended up settling at the confluence of the Saône and the Rhône. In the letters they sent to eachother, Cicero and Munatius Plancus explain that the latter asked the senate's permission to grant plots of land to the veterans to prevent them from rallying Antony's cause. The Senate agreed and added the status of Roman Colony to the area, which meant, among other things, rather advantageous tax status.

Opposite page. In Beaunant, spectacular ruins from the Gier aqueduct. Those are the most important in the region with those of Chaponost.

In Fourvière, rue Roger-Radisson, vestiges from Gier aqueduct, the longest of the four local aqueducts.
In the reign of Augustus, the first two aqueducts were built : that of the Monts d'Or (10,000 square meters of water per day) and that of the Yzeron (13,000 square meters per day).
Claudius had a third aqueduct called 'la Brévenne'. This 66 kilometre giant would bring 28,000 square meters of water to the inhabitants daily.
Under Hadrian, the fourth and longest of the area's aqueducts was built. The Gier aqueduct, with its 85 kilometres of wide canalisations (170 cm in diameter) could feed into town over 25,000 square meters of water a day.

Rue des Farges, in Saint-Just, vestiges of roman thermal baths dating from the first century.

The Fourvière theatre, probably the oldest in France and one of the oldest in the roman world. It was built in 27 BC by emperor Augustus, and Hadrian had it enlarged in 120 AD to accommodate over 10,000. It can nowadays seat over 4,000 people, and a festival called 'Nuits de Fourvière' takes place here in each summer.

Pierre Wuilleumier and Amable Audin have determined the date of the creation of the city thanks to the main axis of the old town. On October 10th, 43 BC, Munatius Plancus traced the *decumanus maximus* - today's *rue Cleberg*, according to Amable Audin – then the *cardo maximus*, the two main perpendicular streets, thus defining the limits of the colony that was to be called Lugdunum. Ethymologically, the name either means town of *Lugus* - Lugus was a Roman god represented by a crow – or '*the hill of light*'. The first coins found to be coined in 43 BC have the drawing of a crow on them.

At that time, the Gauls of the Celtic tribe of the Ségusiaves were occupying the region but were scattered in various locations. Condate, the Gaul borough

The Fourvière odeon, built during the first century, was devoted to music, poetry and public readings.
The magnificent tiling of its orchestra area is a juxtaposition of noble materials: marble from Carrara and Sienna, grey granite and syenite from Italy, green porphyrius from Greece and red from Egypt.

that was set on the Croix-Rousse would only be populated later, after the foundation of Fourvière.

The river people of the Saône settled on the right side of the river. On the island of Canabaes, at the meeting between the Saône and the Rhône (today's Ainay district) the town's trade was made by merchants and settlers.

As it underwent Celtic and eastern influences, the Roman civilisation lost its founding values: family, respect of the Gods, courage, loyalty, fidelity, a certain taste for glory and public situation. That was why Augustus tried to reinstate Roman institutions in 27 BC, with the creation of the worship to the Emperor. He decided that *Lugdunum* would be the capital of the three Gauls and entrusted his son-in-law Agrippa with the creation of the road network departing from the city itself.

Then he asked Drusus, in 12BC, to build the federal sanctuary of the three Gauls. It was the official and compulsory site of imperial worship and the annual meeting place of the representatives of the sixty Gaul tribes.

Thirty one years later, on Tibere's request, Rufus, the priest of Rome and of Augustus, financed the construction cost of the amphitheater of Croix-Rousse where gladiatorial fights and oratory competitions took place. The city already counted 50,000 inhabitants.

Emperor Claudius was born in Lugdunum in 10BC. He is the one who asked the Senate that the inhabitants of the city be granted Roman citizenship in a very famous speech engraved in the bronze works of the Claudian table.

Between the years 117 and 138 in Emperor Hadrien's reign, Lugdunum was at the apex of its glory. The Croix-Rousse amphitheater was extended and could hold 20,000 spectators; the federal sanctuary was also enlarged and two gigantic columns – 14 meters high – were added. A new forum was built on Fourvière Hill as well as the circus and the odeon. Augustus' theater was also extended and could sit 10,000 spectators.

Hadrien started the building of Cybele's sanctuary above Fourvière's theater. Cybele's cult demanded expiatory sacrifices: floggings, bull sacrifices and castrations. Such rituals were later to be replaced by the martyrdom of Christians.

In the middle of the 2nd century, many Christians led by the first bishop, Pothin, settled in Lugdunum. As they believed in a single, loving God, they strongly refused to submit to the official worship which they considered as an abominable apostasy.

They were then looked upon as rebellious citizens whose aim was to jeopardize the emperor's

The whole of the Fourvière archaeological park comprises theatres, the ruins of Cybele's temple, shops, artisans' workshops, a roman road, a water reserve and other life structures like this well.

This is the oldest painted wall in Lyon, it can be found along the road which leads to the archaeological park..

Page Opposite. Mosaics of the circus games, from the end of the second century, found in Ainay in 1806. It shows eight chariots drawn by four horses, and gives us useful clues as to how those games were carried out, but also as to the presence of wooden structures, which have nowadays disappeared. Musée de la Civilisation Gallo-Romaine.

power. Their atheism was said to irritate the gods and they were held responsible for all disasters. They became the scapegoats of a confused society.

In 177, Good Friday clashed with the Cybele celebrations – crowds captured them and terrible acts of torture took place, recorded in the '*Letter of Lyonese Christians to their Asian and Phrygian Brothers*'.

Nineteen were stifled to death in their prison, among whom the bishop Pothin; twenty-four were beheaded because they were Roman citizens and six were fed to beasts among whom Saint Blandine who is said to have tamed the wild beasts and made them lay down at her feet.

A few years later, the emperor Septimus Severius and his general Albinus were at odds on account of Lugdunum itself. The power struggle triggered off reprisals, destructions and pillage which all portended the decline of the city. Roman domination was present until 457 AD, when the Burgunds invaded the town and called it *Lugdon*.

Detail of mosaics and heads of gods of the gallo-roman civilisation. Situated in the archaeological park, the museum presents the richest archaeological collections after those of the Musée National. From the vestiges and objects discovered around Lyon, the museum retraces four centuries of life, costumes, beliefs, art and institutions in Lugdunum.

Under emperor Tiberius, a priest named Rufus built the Croix-Rousse amphitheatre. During Hadrian's reign it was enlarged to seat 20,000. It was the scene of gladiator fights and, in 177, of the death of the Christian martyrs.

In a frame: among the martyrs of 177 AD, Blandine and the bishop Pothin will become the most famed. Detail from the mosaics in the martyrs room in the Antiquaille.

*La Cour des Voraces, n° 9
place Colbert, illuminated
for December 8th.*

The Traboules and Steps of Lyon.

Who hasn't thought, as they walk through the streets of the old town, of the people who used to tread the same historical paths long before them. As a teenager, I used to hang around those narrow streets, and I would be overwhelmed by a feeling of connection with the time of the Renaissance, when the area was all brand new. It was as if the memory locked up in those stones was contracting time and drawing me closer to them.

I used to expect to chance upon them round the corner of one of those narrow footpaths which branch off into covered passageways and interior courtyards, penetrating deep into the recesses of a building to end up in another street altogether.

The word *traboule* comes from the Latin: *trans* which means to cross and *ambulare* which means to move, hence the French verb *trabouler* and the noun traboule. In his study on the architectural particularities of the old town's landscape, René Dejean says that he found out from linguist André Compan that in the old Oc language, the word *travoulo* or *traboulo* means (shortcut).

Such streets are not peculiar to the old town of Lyon. They do happen to be the most ancient around, with the first ones appearing in the fourth century. But the hills of the *Croix-Rousse* are also rich in those architectural gems; the *Canut* silk-workers were in the habit of using them to carry their fabrics out of the rain. The traboules show another aspect of the clandestine nature of the Lyonnais and their penchant for economy.

The diversity of those passages is incredible: ranging from the simple passageway made up of a single

Courtyard at n° 18 rue Saint-Jean. A must-see in the Old Lyon bourgeois style, with its centreless helicoids and its sculpted ogive vaults.

At n° 27 Quai Saint-Antoine, a Presqu'île traboule from the fifteenth to the eighteenth century.

The famous Thiaffait passage, linking the rues Burdeau and Leynaud. Future international centre for haute-couture.

corridor linking two streets together, which is called an *allée* by the locals, to some which use a combination of levels, like the one found *Cour des Voraces*. That particular one is most intriguing; it descends seven floors, follows an alley and crosses two buildings before opening up two streets below. The maze of traboules is so complex that it saved the lives of many Lyonnais people during the French Revolution and during the Second World War.

There are also the courtyards, which were named *miraboules* by Félix Benoit in 1961. Those particular traboules have only one opening and finish up inside a courtyard whose architecture and that of its stairwells are worth admiring (hence, *mirar*).

A thorough census was carried out by specialist René Jean, and over 350 old traboules were counted. As for the beautiful nineteenth and twentieth century ones on the left bank, no one has numbered them yet.

In order to understand what curiosities and architectural riches those traboules are, one has to take the time to walk down one or two. One can even push a door here and there to check if an *allée* is hiding on the other side, but remember to respect the privacy of their owners. Most of those areas are open to the public only under the condition that tourists will remain courteous.

Lyon's Steps

We will not discuss here the superb covered stairwells which snake their way up the Renaissance towers in the Old Town. The steps in question are to be found on *Fourvière* and Croix-Rousse, whose topography force their inhabitants to create shortcuts on the slopes themselves with steps going straight or sideways, sometimes breathtakingly steeply. Fourvière counts eleven of them, Croix-Rousse thirty-five, but if one counts the actual amount of steps, Fourvière gets the prize. In Croix-Rousse, the *rue Grognard* climbs a mere 200 steps in three successive flights. In Fourvière, it is not an easy feat to climb down the 435 steps of the *montée du Greillon*, let alone climb up! But then one can also reach the metallic tower from the *Saint-Paul* railway station: just climb up the *Carmes Déchaussées* hill and carry on up the *Nicolas de Lange* hill. A mere 800 steps, but what a benefit for one's calves!

Two magnificent flights of steps descending from place Chardonnet.

Rue Grognard would you believe!

Renaissance Lyon

The Old Town reveals the splendour of fifteenth and sixteenth century Lyon. It comprises, from North to South, the *Saint-Paul*, *Saint-Jean* and *Saint-Georges* areas.

This area of town knows how to seduce those who are discovering it for the first time.

A visitor reaching *Bellecour* in the morning would stand spellbound at the sight of its ochre and pink facades as they are reflected into the Saône in hues of amber and honey.

A village within the city, the *Vieux-Lyon* nestles at the foot of the Fourvière mount : all in all, it spans thirty-five hectares of old dwellings, twenty-four of which are listed buildings. It is the largest Renaissance site in France, and the second in Europe after Venice. From the belvedere of the Basilica, the vista encompasses the multicoloured tones of its Roman-style tiled roofs, and the numerous Renaissance towers which punctuate this majestic sight.

But as bewitching as the Vieux-Lyon looks at first sight, it gains much more still from being experienced on foot, as one strolls through its maze of narrow paved streets.

Squeezed between the Fourvière hill and the Saône river: Vieux-Lyon.

In 1964, the district was the first in France to be granted the title of *secteur sauvegardé* (preserved area) by the Malraux Ministry. The *Renaissance du Vieux Lyon' association*, hard at work since the 1950s, has played a major role in the classification of these districts and successfully opposed attempts to destroy them under various town planning or public health pretexts.

How did the Vieux-Lyon develop into gem that it is today? In 1436, King Louis XI allowed free fairs to be held, which in turn attracted wealthy merchants and bankers from all the surrounding nations, particularly from Italy.

At the same time, the King and his court often stayed in the city. Silk weaving was promoted by the successive kings of France, Louis XI and Francis I. The

One of the gems of Vieux-Lyon: the Mayet de Beauvoir house built in 1516. But who decides what is a gem in a site packed with wonders?

Place du Change. At its centre, draper Thomassin's house with its twin mullion windows (1493).

At no. 2 rue Saint-Georges, a magnificent stairwell curls up into an ellipse.

city also became the capital of printing, as it was developed there by Bartholomew Buyer. Many artists, scholars and poets used to gather around the bookshops and contributed to the creative cultural enrichment of the period.

This was a very prosperous era, promoting the construction of sumptuous Gothic or Renaissance abodes, full of that peculiar character defined today as the Lyonnais style. They all share a rather plain exterior and luxurious courtyards and interiors. A certain spirit of competition was instituted as to who

Hôtel Croppet at 14 rue du Bœuf, with its splendid archways built in 1467.

Spectacular archways in the alley of no. 20 rue Juiverie.

At no. 58 rue Saint-Jean, a particularly interesting Renaissance well, opened on three sides with three shell ceilings.

would build the most beautiful courtyard, the most original staircase tower or the most elaborate arcade galleries. The *Hôtel Bullioud* (designed by Philibert de l'Orme in 1536) is the undisputed winner with a beautiful gallery counter-buttressed by two penditive turrets. In fact, it is the patent signature of the Renaissance French masons.

All the houses were built on the same plan. Their two separate wings are parallel to the street and joined by a courtyard, with a staircase tower to enable people to reach the different floors through the open arcade galleries, sometimes even a belvedere with a vegetable garden and some stables, a peculiar feature which particularly impressed Rabelais.

Some people see the influence of the Florentine style in this district. Despite the fact that by the end of the 16th century two-thirds of foreigners living in Lyon resided next to the *Place du Change* (Stock Exchange Square), their presence did not influence the style of the houses. Their wealth enabled them to build large and luxurious edifices but they chose to stick to the existing architectural style.

Some particularly splendid examples should be visited:

Saint John's Cathedral is the heart of the district and Saint Paul's collegiate church is the oldest religious building.

Saint George's Church, built in the neo-Gothic style was constructed in 1844 by Bossan, who used to call it a youthful indiscretion. It is currently the parish used by traditionalist Catholics.

At no. 22 rue Juiverie, Baronat House. Named after the rich bourgeois family who owned it from 1446 to 1538. Corner towers, window sills resting on sculpted figures. Basket-handle arches with overhanging heads sculpted into the stone. In the courtyard are four galleries, which were made by the same hand as the Maison des Avocats.

At no. 42 rue Saint-Jean, beautiful fifth century house, with double archway galleries opening out onto an interior courtyard.

Cour des Loges. Prestigious Hôtel set in the old outbuildings of the Petit Collège des Jésuites. Then became the laboratory of the mage Philippe de Lyon (1849-1905), the thaumaturgist rival of Rasputin at the Russian Court.

Hostellerie du Gouvernement, place du Gouvernement, fifteenth century. Detail from a doorway.

As far as secular architecture is concerned, no one can overlook the likes of :

The *Grand Palais des Laurencins* - cloth merchants in the *Rue St Jean* – and its octagonal tower.

The *Maison des Avocats, Rue de la Bombarde*, a.k.a. *Cour de la Basoche*, is a fine example of successful renovation.

The *Maison du Cribble, Rue du Bœuf*, is famous for its rose tower. The *Loge du Change*, situated *Place du Change*, was enlarged in 1747 by Soufflot and aimed at accommodating money changers when fairs took place.

The *Hôtel Paterin*, locally known as the Henri IV style house, displays three floors of galeries and a superb scrolled staircase.

Vieux-Lyon is no museum though. Just walk around and look out for mullion windows, basket-handle doors, traboules with intersecting rib vaults, spiral staircases and towers, streets or plazas. The *Place de La Trinité* traboule, for example, at the bottom of the *Gourguillon* Rise will forever remain famous because of the Punch and Judy show that took place in the *Maison du Soleil* (the House of the Sun) right across the plaza.

This historic district also has its own museum housed within the spacious *Hôtel de Gadagne*. The Old Lyon is a lively place where artists and craftsmen like to meet and exhibit their work, every Sunday, at the *Saint-George* Art Market.

Maison des Avocats. Old Auberge de la Croix-d'Or, fondée en 1471.

Lyon and Silk Weaving

Back in the Middle Ages, silk weaving already evoked prestige and luxury, but importing the fabric was draining France's resources. So in 1466 King Louis XI intended to create a factory in order to manufacture gold and silk fabric within his realm. But the political alliance of the Lyon Consulate with influent Italian bankers and merchants living in Lyon who traded with Italy brought the project to an end.

Francis I wanted to ruin Genoa's economy on account of their support of Charles Quint, his rival. In 1515, he grew aware of Lyon's commercial growth – it was the base of his Italian conquests – and of the trading value of silk in his kingdom. He then renewed Charles VIII's order forbidding the use of foreign silk and issued a decree in favour of foreign weavers settling in his kingdom and exempting them from tax.

Georges Matelon is an authentic Croix-Rousse Canut.

From that moment on, the Consulate's attitude changed. In 1536, two Genoese weavers, Etienne Turquet and Barthélemy Nariz were allowed to install mechanical looms in the Saint-George district. In 1540, the King issued another order declaring that Lyon was to be '*the only repository storing any kind of silk entering the kingdom.*'

In 1554, the Union of Workers who made '*fabrics made out of gold, silver and silk*' was created for the 12,000 odd silk workers of the area. But the quality of the silk produced was not on a par with the Italian material. In 1606, Lyonnais weaver Claude Dangon perfected a loom which at last enabled the long-awaited manufacture of large designed fabrics.

Pages 52 and 53, the 'à la grande tire' loom, on which Jean-Yves, weaver at the Maison des Canuts, demonstrates ancient techniques.

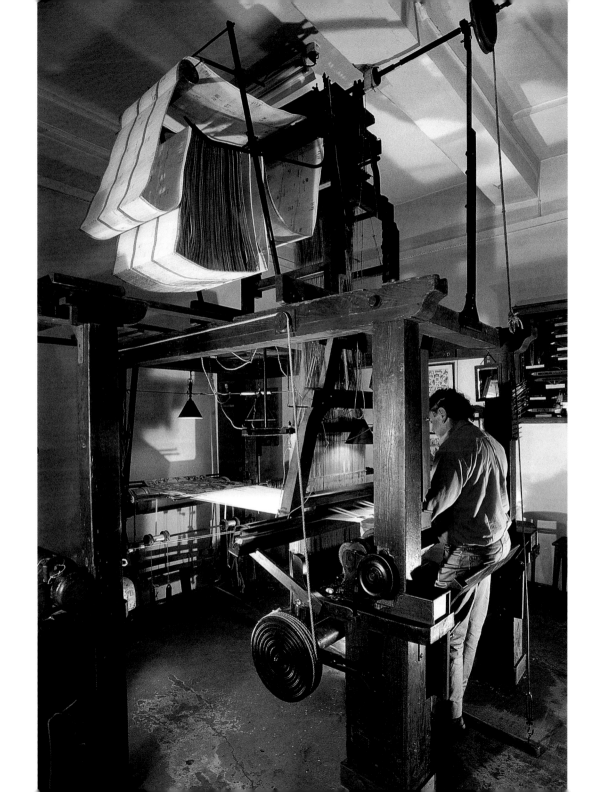

Place de la Croix-Rousse, statue of Jacquard, sculpted by Elie Ottavry in 1947.

In 1667, Colbert, a minister of King Louis XIV, mentored the companies representing French know-how and founded the *Grande Fabrique*, a trade union which brought together all the silk traders and determined quality criteria.

Lyon started to have its own original style developed by local designers. But, just when Lyon's fame was reaching the world's stage, came the revocation of the Nantes Edict which forced into exile all the

It is a yellow-stoned cross which gave its name to the 'Croix-Rousse' area.

At the Maison des Canuts, Eric works with a Jacquard loom.

Hand painted fruits and leaves on silk muslin.

protestant bankers, makers and weavers, reducing the number of working looms in the city from 13,000 to 4,000. But the town's trade returned to normal and a new style expanded under the influence of the flower painters from the Gobelins and the Savonnerie school. A Lyonnais school of design came to life in 1756.

Twenty-four draughtsmen worked in Lyon in 1790, the most famous of whom being Philippe de Lasalle who was at the same time an ingenious inventor, weaver, merchant and mechanic.

Thanks to the Lyon input, French style became renowned all over the world.

But the Canut silk workers were still living in miserable conditions and they grew increasingly bitter. Wanting their talents to be recognised, they demonstrated in 1744 and 1786. But the demonstrations went unheeded, and developed into riots. After the French Revolution, feeling cheated, they gave up the fight. Many manufacturers went their separate ways and numerous workshops closed down. Out of 18,000 looms in 1787 only 2,000 were running in 1793.

In 1804, Joseph Marie Jacquard designed, using Vaucanson's work, a new weaving loom which could increase productivity with the use of punch card programming. Because of the size of those new looms, the making of silk was transferred to Croix-Rousse, which thus became '*the Working Hill*'.

In 1831, 6,000 Canuts demonstrated in favour of a minimum wage. The city's Prefect gave them the go-ahead as the merchants did not follow suit and refused to pay them, and the fight went on. Brandishing their black flags, the Canuts shouted their famous slogan: '*vivre en travaillant ou mourrir*

One of Lyon's artists, Shou Sundara, paints local landscapes on silk.

At the Maison des Canuts, Eric demonstrates the use of a mechanical loom.

en combatant' (we'll earn a living or fight to the death). Some of the workers, called *Voraces*, were libertarian social democrats who also took part in the 1848 Revolution.

Despite this unrest, the number of looms kept increasing. There were 60,000 of them in 1848 and the record was even broken in 1853 with a 2,200-ton production of raw silk.

Two years later, a terrible silkworm infestation ravaged French silk-farms. Pasteur did work out a remedy but the damage was done and half the used silk had to be imported. Industrialisation was on its way and the appearance of synthetic fibres gave the silk industry a finishing stroke. Still, in 1930, a new printing technique called *à la Lyonnaise* was invented and silkscreen printing replaced block printing.

Today all the looms are modernised, computerized and air-jet run, yet only 350 tons of silk are still produced in Lyon. A few prestigious workshops manufacture hand-made silk to keep the old techniques of the Canut workers alive: in fact, they are the ones who carry out the orders of the Historic Monuments or of the most famous Haute Couture designers.

The *Maison des Canuts*, situated in the *Rue d'Ivry*, has become a museum which re-enacts Lyon's silk weaving traditions. Two Canut workers weave in front of visitors and give explanations. If you visit the *Musée des Tissus*, you will be able to admire centuries of Lyonese silk. A new association called *Soie Vivante* (living silk) puts into use the old looms in actual Canut workshops. Many designers and craftsmen still make hand-painted and Lyonnais printed silk.

The Association Soierie Vivante, rue Richan, exhibits three magnificent working braiding-looms.

Charlemagne's crown, detail of a mantelpiece from the twelfth century abbey on the Île de Barbe. Musée Historique de la ville de Lyon.

Hidden behind the Black Virgin chapel, the Chapelle du Voeu of 1643, sadly still shut to the public.

Lyon, religious city

The history of the Lyonese church is deeply rooted in the early years of Christendom since St John's disciple Saint Polycarp, bishop of Smyrna, and his own disciple, Saint Pothin, who became the first bishop of Lyon. The Lyon Church acquired its prestige with the matyrdom of Saint Blandine, Bishop Pothin and their companions, in the Three Gauls' amphitheater on the *Croix-Rousse* Hill, in the year 177. That sacrifice will earn Lyon the title of 'primatiale' of the Gauls, which is where the highest ranking archbishop would hold his ministry.

Saint Irénée, Lyon's second bishop after Saint Pothin in 177, was the first person to speak of an Immaculate Conception. His works on Gnosis earned him worldwide fame.

A great many monuments relate the chronicle of Lyon's Christians and of their worship to the Virgin Mary.

One finds even lay examples of this particular devotion, in the *Hôtel-Dieu* hospital built in 549 under her protection, or in the General Alms House, created in 1533.

Three hundred and fifty Madonnas are displayed over many street corners and fifty nine churches witness to the faith of the inhabitants of the city throughout the ages.

In the middle of the river Saône, the vestiges of the Île Barbe abbey.

Modern acropolis, the Fourvière basilica toers over the city.

completely and September 8th became one of the great religious celebrations in Lyon.

After Napoleon III's defeat in 1870 and upon the request of the Lyonese ladies, Bishop Ginoulhiac solemnly promised to the Virgin Mary that, if the Prussians did not invade Lyon, a sanctuary would be built on Fourvière Hill. A great number of the city's inhabitants formally sign that declaration. His wish was granted: the Prussians did not heed their orders and walked away from Lyon and the city was saved. Subscriptions were launched, every stone of the future edifice could be bought, and the individual sponsors's number engraved into the stone. Many families took to visiting Fourvière to watch their stone being laid, and later to visit the site.

Architect Pierre Bossan supervised the building of the chapel in 1872, and it was consecrated in 1896 by Cardinal Couillé. Bossan was influenced by mystical painter Louis Janmot, and therefore saw the sanctuary on Fourvière as '*the palace of the most powerful of queens…*', the *Turris davidica* of the Virgin Mary's litanies. So, the symbol is illustrated by the fact that the angels of the façade are armed with swords and those inside the basilica are peaceful musicians.

The neobyzantine decoration of sculptures, gildings and colours is devoted to Mary's life and is a reminder her importance within France's history and the world. The symbol of the intermediary role of the Mother of Christ was illustrated in architectural terms and in the decoration of the site.

Many other churches are worth a close look.

Saint Martin-d'Ainay is the oldest church in Lyon and the only Romanesque building since the destruction of the Island of Barbe's abbey whose tym-

Many events seem to have encouraged and reinforced this profound faith.

In the 17th century, the plague was devastating the population. The merchants' provost and the city's aldermen decided to call on the Virgins help. They vowed to erect two statues in Her honour and to walk in procession for Her every year '… *to attend mass, pray to the Virgin and offer her 7 pounds of white wax… and a gold coin to the sun…*'. The plague disappeared

The Saint-Martin d'Ainay basilica could do with a facelift.

panum were incorporated into the newer edifice. The original decor and the porch-like spire are some of the most interesting elements of the façade.

Inside, the four pillars that surround the transept were taken from the old altar to Rome and to Augustus which had been erected on the Croix-Rousse hill in 12 BC. In the semicircular cupola vault of the choir, Hippolyte Flandrin painted Christ blessing the Virgin Mary, Blandine, Clothilde and Pothin on a golden mosaic backdrop.

The Romanesque sculpture of the cornices and of the chancel of the *Saint-Martin* church compete with those of the most famous churches around.

Saint John the Baptist's *primatiale* church was erected in the 12th century to replace the three churches whose vestiges can be seen in the archeological garden nearby. It was started in the Romanesque style, continued through the Gothic period and finally ended in the Flamboyant style. Its seventeenth century façade is most remarkable with its rose formed by

Like Medieval Mysteries before them, the Pennons celebrations take place on the cathedral's steps.

Some of the hundreds of medallions of the façade of the cathedral.

Graphic details from the Manécanterie facade.

six trefoil circles set in a six petal flower and its three hundred and twenty sculpted medallions. Two hundred of these medallions were unfortunately destroyed by Huguenots in 1562 together with 50 statues. The astronomical clock from the sixteenth and seventeenth centuries still chimes on the hour four times a day.

Next door, the Romanesque façade of the Cathedral's twentieth century singing school (called *la manécanterie* after the Latin *manne cantare* meaning morning singing) hides the gem which is the Cathedral.

Two Catholic Councils took place in the Cathedral, as well as the wedding of King Henri IV with Queen Margot on 13 December 1600.

Seen from the heights of Fourvière, the imposing mass of the cathedral and its curiously off-centre southern tower.

The venerable old Astronomical Clock still rings four times a day.

The Bourbons chapel with its exceptionally flamboyant gothic style.

On the Croix-Rousse hill, the former Chartreuse du Lys du Saint Esprit chapel, now known as Saint Bruno's church is a Baroque work of art. The baldaquin of the chancel surmounted by a magnificent canopy designed in 1738 by the Italian artist, Servandoni, overlooks the double faced orange marble altar by Soufflot.

Saint Paul's church is a juxtaposition of Roman and Gothic styles. Several remarkable sections date back to the twelfth century: Saint Laurent's door, the projecting ornaments around the roof edges and the hexagonal cupola decorated with a two-tier blind arcade. Others date back to the Gothic era, particularly interesting is the chapel with its arch curve, ornamented with medallions featuring choirs of angels.

Opposite the church is the statue Jean Charlier, well-known theologian who supported Joan of Arc. He was chancellor at the Université de Paris and died in 1429, Saint Paul's canon in Lyon after having dedicated his life to the education of the young.

Next to Saint Irénée's church and its crypt to the martyrs, Saint Irénée's Calvary is the last of its kind to dominates the city.

Dating back to the early days of Christianity, the Lyonnais mass is one a great traditional ritual. When Pope Pius V permanently codified the Roman ritual, he did not erase the two hundred previous years of rituals. It is thus still possible to hear mass in Latin in the specifically Lyon style.

Many saints walked the streets of the city in their time. Some, like Saint Bonaventure or saint Francis of Sales died there. Many Lyonnais actualy spread the faith abroad.

In 1699, Charles Démia founded the first school for poor children.

Angels playing music, a constant image in Saint-Paul's church.

Behind the cathedral, the vestiges of three ancient churches are gathered in the Jardin Archéologique Girard Desargues.

Saint Nizier's church, an odd looking but pleasing façade. A gem of the baroque period was placed there: a statue of Our Lady of Grace sculpted by Coysevox in 1674. Dating from the fifteenth century, it is worth a look for its two dissimilar steeples (one from the fifteenth and the other from the nineteenth century), as well as its curious 1549 clock decorating the vault of the nave.

Pauline Jaricot (1799 – 1862) was the founder of the movement for the propagation of the faith and of the workers' religious actions. Her Living Rosary counted some two million members throughout the world.

Claudine Thévenet (1775-1836), founder of the Jesus-Mary Congregation and the Providence Institution, took care of abandonned girls. She was canonized in 1993.

The Vierge de Coysevox, copied so many times.

Saint-Nizier, a beautiful gothic nave filled with light.

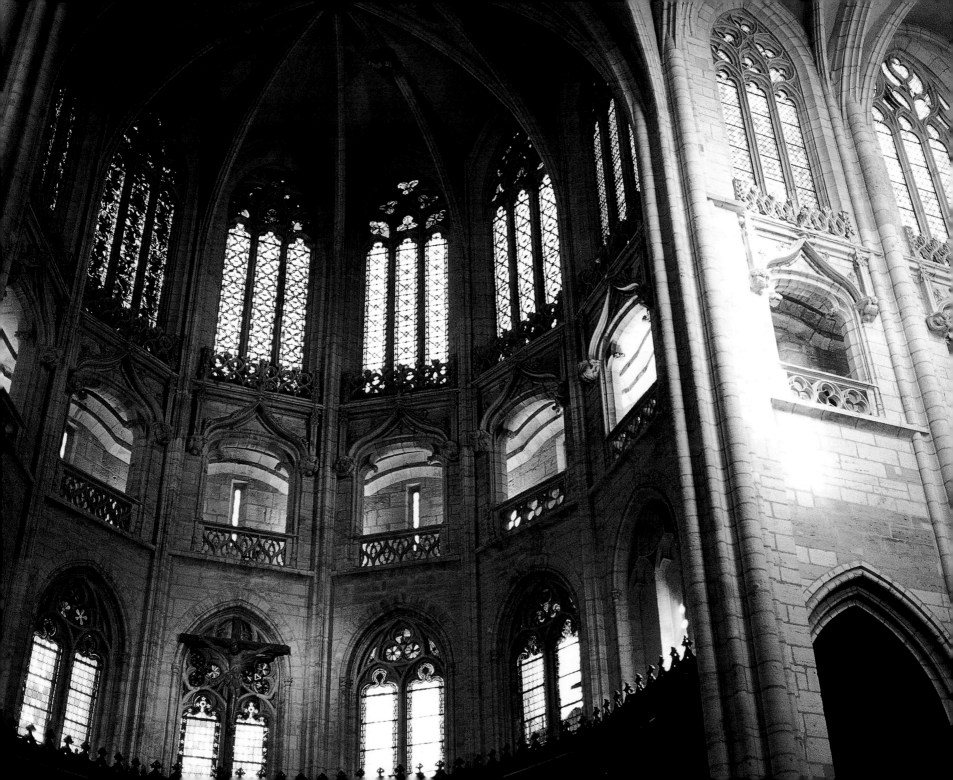

Saint-François-de-Sales, neoclassical church rich in relics of Saint Francis. The cupola's frescoes are by Louis Janmot (1859), the furniture by J.-H. Fabisch and the font comes from Sainte-Marie-Perrin.

Bishop de Marion Brésillac launched the African Missions in 1856.

Cardinal Gerlier, the archbishop of Lyon during the second World War, stood up to the Nazis and saved a great many Jews and members of the French Resistance.

Frédéric Ozanam created Saint Vincent de Paul's conferences, and Father Chevrier founded the Prado Institution to help workers in 1864. He was one of the renowned socially-conscious Catholics together with Bishop de Bonald, precursor of Christian workers' Unions.

The surprising archway in Saint-Just church.

The double faced altar made out of orange marbe by Soufflot for Saint-Bruno baroque church.

Servandoni's canopy for Saint-Bruno, dating from 1738.

In the Basilica, a mosaic commemorates the link between December 8th 1854 and December 8th 1852.

The origin of the celebrations came with this golden Virgin by Fabisch. Her hands are disproportionately large so as to be seen from the banks of the Saône.

City of Light

After the city's aldermen prayed long and hard for the plague to disappear, their wish seemed finally granted in 1643, and September 8th became a Lyonnais celebration. The date was chosen in 1852 to bless and inaugurate the large bronze gilded statue of the Virgin Mary placed on the dome of the city's new steeple. The statue, which is six-meters high, was designed by Fabisch who also sculpted the statue of the Miraculous Virgin Mary that can be seen in Lourdes.

Unfortunately, the workshop where the statue was kept was flooded by the Saône river, thus postponing the ceremony until December 8th.

On that day, despite the dreadful weather, the general mood was ecstatic. The ringing of the bells and booming of the canons could be heard for miles around. Cardinal de Bonald blessed the gilded statue, and at that very moment, a terrible storm broke out, forcing the crowds to run for shelter. The ceremony was interrupted and the bonfire was cancelled.

A few hours later, however, the wind and rain stopped. The people, deprived of their celebration, came back into the streets and started lighting fires to light up the Fourvière chapel and the new statue. Millions of candles were placed on the window sills of all the city's façades. On impulse people stated meeting in the streets and celebrations went on all through the night. The *Fête des lumières* of December 8th was born.

Two years later, on December 8th 1854, Pope Pius IX proclaimed the dogma of the Immaculate Conception, which Lyon's second bishop, Saint-Irenee, had first discussed in his works. On that day, many Lyonese felt their faith strengthened by the belief that God had chosen Lyon to pay homage to His Mother.

Nowadays, the Fête des Lumières, created to replace the celebration of December 8th, has lost all religious connotation. Only a few fervent Catholics still walk in procession through the garden of the Rosary on that day.

At the end of the 80's, the municipality of Lyon grew aware of the incredible trump card that these lights represented and how they could put their monuments into better focus thanks to adapted lighting.

Celebratory blue robes for the Basilica. Next to it, in gigantic lights, the declaration: 'Ave Maria'.

Festival des lumières 2000, the Jacobins fountain is illuminated.

Working on a project entitled '*Lyon, the City of Lights*', the town council wanted to prove that the use of these lights would enrich the city's architectural scene from an aesthetic point of view. Since 1999, more than two hundred and sixty seven monuments, twenty facades and twenty streets are illuminated every night. For the 10th anniversary commemorating the Project of Lights, on December 8th 1999, the lighting was exceptional. That night, Lyon was called '*World Capital of Lights*'.

Today the town is proud of its title, and it now exports its lighting expertise to many countries like Saint Petersburg, Havana or even Ho Chi Minh City.

Festival des lumières 1999, the 'Cité Internationale' is in a showing-off mood.

Festival des lumières 1999, the town hall has come out as Harlequin.

Lyon's Monuments

When Lyon became a World Heritage Site, Unesco experts were impressed by the readability of historic periods across the city's monuments. Those monuments can be classified chronologically. Leaving aside Roman or religious buildings, we will have a look at the city's monuments in order of their creation.

In the twelfth century began the construction of the *Hôtel-Dieu*. It was intended to extend the existing hospital built in 549 by the bishop Saint Sacerdos, upon the request of King Childebert of the Burgonds and Queen Ultrogoth, to provide free medical care for pregnant women without resources and the needy.

The Lyon tradition of charity was then born which served as a model for other communities and was strengthened in 1665 with the creation of the Community of the Sisters of Charity.

After the French Revolution, the town council joined up the Hôtel-Dieu and the hospital of Charity founded in 1617 by the General Alms, thus forming Lyon's public hospital.

The Hôtel-Dieu cloister, around which the names of the public hospitals sponsors are engraved. A plaque also commemorates Rabelais medical work there from 1532 to 1535.

Musée des Hospices Civils: statue of Saint Clair.

Musée des Hospices Civils : an impressive collection of chemist's pots from all periods.

Musée des Hospices Civils presents hospital life through many object and works of Art. It holds numerous apothecary items from Hôtel-Dieu and Hopital de la Charité (photo opposite). Above, a detail of the woodwork in the Charité featuring a tooth puller.

Lyon's town hall on the Terreaux square.

The town hall's red salon.

Construction of Simon Maupin's Town Hall started in 1646 in the purest Louis XIII style. It was partly destroyed by fire on 13 September 1672, but Jules-Hardouin Mansart, Louis XIV's architect, restored it in 1699.

The Town Hall does not lack interest: the equestrian statue of Henri IV was designed by sculptor Legendre-Héral in 1827; the belfry shelters a sixty-five bell carillon and a 1914 clock which chimes the hours on a 2.1 ton bell and repeats them on another 4.3 ton bell. The famous *boule d'or* (gold ball), often mistaken for a barometer, is in fact an astronomical clock made in 1652, which served as an astrolab indicating the different phases of the moon.

It is the home of a surprising three-eyed Cyclops, designed by sculptor Lucien Pascal in 1883.

The main stairway is entirely painted with an allegory by Thomas Blanchet.

The *Palais Saint Pierre* situated on *Place des Terreaux* is a fine example of Italian Baroque style. It used to be the convent of the Canoness Ladies of Saint Pierre. Demolished by the Huguenots in 1562, the abbey was rebuilt in 1686 according to the plans of architect Royer de la Valnefière.

After a thorough renovation program, the building now hosts the Museum of Fine Arts of Lyon which displays some of the greatest collections of French works with French, Spanish, Flemish, Italian and Dutch paintings but also some of the works from the 19th century Lyonnais school. 14,500 square meters of exhibitions cover paintings, sculptures, Egyptian, Greek and Roman antiquities, and an important collection of decorative art. The Palais Saint-Pierre is so rich in varied works of art that it is the largest French museum outside Paris.

Opposite, the stairwell decorated by Thomas Blanchet in the town hall.

In the gardens of the Musée des Beaux-Arts, bronzes by Carpeau, Rodin, Bourdelle, and others meet up for a chat.

The new layout of the Musée Saint-Pierre, for a better appreciation of the works.

The temple of the Reformed Church (1803) used to be the Loge du Change. It evokes the role played by the merchant bankers who settled in the Old Lyon from the sixteenth century. As the seventeenth century construction turned out to be too small, the town's Consulate asked Soufflot to enlarge it in 1748.

In 1595, Pré Bellecourt was transformed into a square upon Henri IV's request. It was later enlarged by Louis XIV and a statue of the King designed by Desjardins was placed there in 1713, together with the statues of the Coustou brothers representing the Saône and Rhône rivers. The King's statue was unfor-

La loge du Change, reworked by Soufflot.

Place Bellecour, the second statue of Louis XIV by Lemot, in 1825. The two allegories of the Rhône and the Saône by the Coustou brothers date from the older statue of 1713.

tunately melted under the Revolution in order to make cannons, so a new statue was created by Lyonnais sculptor Lemot. Bonarparte later had the square restored after the damage they had endured during the Convention.

Situated in Place de la Comédie, the Grand Théatre by Germain Soufflot was opened in 1756.

Inside, the architecture was rather modern for the times, with its oval-shaped room and three retreating galleries. From 1827 to 1831, architects Pollet and Chenavard gave it the character we knew until 1997, but it was then transformed by architect Jean Nouvel and was given a metallic dome, which the Lyonese nicknamed *grill pain* (Toaster).

The Théatre des Celestins was built on an old Celestine convent in 1407. It was rebuilt in 1877 by Lyonese architect Gaspard André and is one of the last Italian-type theatres in France.

Laid out round the room in the shape of a horse-shoe, the tiered galleries can be reached through a large atrium decorated with antique masks. The luxurious decoration and the red and gold colours high-

Magestic Théatre des Célestins by Gaspard André.

light the spirit of the end of the 19th century. Two hundred and fifty thousand spectators flock there each year to attend the half-classical, half-innovative programme chosen by Director Jean-Paul Lucet.

The *Palais de Justice* (Law Court) was built in 1835, where the former prison of Roanne had once stood. It was nicknamed '*24 pillars*' and was designed by Louis-Pierre Baltard who found his inspiration in the Greco-Roman style, in vogue at the time. The façade, composed of 24 Corynthian columns, defines a long disproportionate peristyle which dominates the entire building. The edifice was heavily cri-ticized at

Grand-Théâtre, now Opera House, with its 'toaster' top by Jean Nouvel.

The Halle, masterpiece by Tony Garnier in the nineteenth century, a gem of the futuristic Gerland area.

Despite the tribunal's move out, the 24 Colonnes still house the High Court and County Court.

the time. Today, it is used as the Court of Appeal and Assize Court.

The *Palais du Commerce* (Trading Palace) which was built in 1860, gathers the sections of the Chamber of Commerce and Industry of Lyon. One of its most remarkable features is the stockbroker's central enclosure of the former stock exchange. The painted ceiling, supported by caryatids, displays a magnificent allegory.

The *Préfecture* (Governor's house) and the *Conseil Général du Rhône* (County Council) were built in 1890 by architect Antonin Louvier. The staircase is monumental and many salons store numerous works of art. The Debating Room is flooded in light through the glass roof designed by Lucien Bégule.

The *Tony Garnier* Market, which used to be the *Mouche* slaughter-house, is the largest covered surface in Europe where no posts are used to support the weight of its roof. It rests on metallic beams erected on ball and socket joints, 120 meters high. It can house 18,000 people.

Tony Garnier, an architect with a vision, winner of the *Grand Prix de Rome*, designed other buildings in Lyon such as the *Grange-Blanche* Hospital, the Stadium of *Gerland*, and his Cité Ideale, partially built in the American district.

Errors of judgement made in the 1960s resulted in the building of the *Cour de Verdun* (which will be demolished in 2006), and the flash construction of the *Part-Dieu* district whose aim was to create a second city-centre because the *Presqu'île* Peninsula was over-populated. The 'Crayon' (the Crédit Lyonnais 170 meter tower) sticks out a mile; the public library is a kind of silo supposed to store two million books;

In the Palais du Commerce, the imposing traders room.

the auditorium for Lyon's national orchestra is gigantic; not to mention the modern *TGV* railway station.

At the end of the last century, the ambition was to create quality areas such as the *Place des Terreaux* or the *Cité Internationale* designed by architect Renzo Piano, built on the former site of the Fair. The Conference Hall, a cinema, a Hilton hotel and the Museum of Modern Art and a casino can be found there, next to Interpol Headquarters.

The first stage of the Cité Internationale by architect Renzo Piano.

Musée d'Art Contempora

The first ever Guignol, sculpted by Laurent Mourguet. Musée de la Marionnette.

At the Musée de la Marionnette, Mourguet and three of his characters. 1908.

Guignol

Laurent Mourguet, creator of *Guignol*, was born in Lyon to a family of Canut workers in 1769. He was brought up learning the weaving trade.

Around 1797, unemployed like many fellow Canuts, he became a professional tooth-puller and in the tradition of the profession, he would attract customers by putting on a little puppet show presenting Italian *Commedia dell'arte* classics. As he felt more drawn to the theater than to the art of dentistry, he created his own theatre where parts of his show wandered into the grounds of current affairs satire. He would never let go of this trait which would later enable his Guignol shows to display his irreverent humour.

He teamed up with a very popular comedian of the time called Lambert Grégoire Ladré, also called Father Thomas, who was a puns and spoof expert. Both knew that they would not be successful if they simply relied on Italian puppets. However, quarrels soon broke up the twosome, Father Thomas was a very short-tempered man! In order to replace him, Mourguet found a much more amenable companion: he made a rather jolly puppet with a glib tongue, which he called Gnafron. Its name is derived from the Lyonnais word *gnaffre* which means shoemaker. *Gnafron* was a rather colourful character, dressed in a leather apron, and a top hat, with a red face and a puffy nose inherited from his love of Beaujolais wine.

Still, Mourguet had not struck gold. He could not attract the punters, so he got a job at the Crèche Brunet, a theatre with string marionettes. There, he discovered the essence of puppet shows, as he played the role of Father Coquart, a no-nonsense, popular,

At the Guignol Theatre in the old town, puppets now look much more sophisticated.

happy-go-lucky character who would later inspire him to create the famous Guignol.

In 1808, he sculpted a puppet to whom he gave his own round face, mischievous eyes and his funny little turned up nose. He dressed him like Father Coquart, in the Canut fashion of the day: i. e. in a brown jacket adorned with golden buttons and a red bow-tie. On his head, he put a soft leather hat with turned down ear-flaps on his *sarsifis*, which means a braid of hair tied with a ribbon.

Why did he call him Guignol? More than two centuries after his creation, no one knows the answer

An eye-catching individual project: le Petit Musée de Guignol, chez Design Cardelli, rue Saint-Jean.

A scene from the classic repertoire: the tooth-puller. At the Guignol of the Madame Moritz Park.

An old puppet theatre at the Musée de la Marionnette.
J. Grateloup, 1896.

The famous wall dedicated to Guignol in the Vieux-Lyon, rue Carrand.

and more than ten different explanations have been put forward but it seems impossible to decide which is accurate.

Mourguet then created other characters and acquired a certain fame with the performances he gave of Guignol in its definitive satirical parody version, in the Café-Théâtre. But beyond comedy, with his rather straightforward morals and his bantering habits, Guignol denounced injustice and become the spokesman of the poor and the needy. Armed with the stick he called '*tavelle, clarinette à faire danser les ours ou la racine d'Amérique'* (clarinet to make bears dance or American root), Guignol delivers justice. As Louis Jacquemin once wrote: '*He fooled the rich and the mighty, beat Policemen, scoffed at the landlord, the solicitor and even the judge...'* Such is the mischievous and independent spirit of Guignol, and this explains why he is still so popular two centuries later.

This delicious crayfish quenelle with Nantua sauce can be enjoyed at Lucien Rabatel's restaurant « la Voûte ».

Cervelas with truffles by Colette Sibilla.

Lyon's Gastronomy

Maurice Edmond Sailland, a.k.a. Curnonsky, established Lyon as the world capital of gastronomy: '*it deserves that name*', he said, '*because here, coo-king reaches the apex of any Art, that is to say: simpli-city*'. In Lyon, indeed, cooking is an art and a chef is more of a philosopher than a technician. For him, eating is a type of worship.

This abundance of foods gave birth to all kinds of Lyonnais specialities, be it the *Mères* – mothers –, the *bouchons* – popular little restaurants – or a multitude of rituals and products.

Lyon's Mères are inherited from the nineteenth century. After the French revolution, the cooks of the great bourgeois houses were encouraged, by their masters, to create their own recipes and write them down on copybooks. Some of them, taking advantage of their skills, opened their own restaurants. Some, like

Some traditional dishes one can find in the bouchons, at Arlette Hugon's.

Colette Sibilla, the most famous charcutière in Lyon.

Eugénie Brazier, were fortunate enough to be awarded three stars in the prestigious *Michelin guide*. One Paul Bocuse spent 1946 as an apprentice in her establishment. Those '*Mothers*' were the trainers of today's great chefs, and their cuisine placed Lyon and France as the leaders in the art of eating.

The Bouchons are peculiar guardians of Lyon's gastronomic traditions. Their name comes from Ancient Rome, but the restaurants themselves first appeared in the nineteenth century. There, you will eat the type of food that the Mères and the Canuts used to cook. In a traditional bouchon, all the dishes are placed on the red and white checked tablecloth at the same time and the chef often is a rough looking fellow whose spirit seems alive with a certain type of Rabelaisian wit.

A *mâchon* is a typically Lyonnais meal. According to Félix Benoît: '*A mâchon is not any kind of meal. It is some sort of snack that can be taken either around 9 a.m. to pass the time, or around 5 p.m. to avoid starving before dinner*'. It is composed of hot pork meat such as pork rinds but also of various kinds of *saucisson*, of *grattons* (scratchings) and sometimes salads where you will find *clapotons* (donkey snout), *pieds de moutons* (mutton foot), *dandelions* and *béatilles* (giblets).

Since the Gauls, Lyon's specialty is its charcuterie, among which you will find the famous *saucisson de Lyon*. Its label demands 100 % pork meat and specially diced fat.

The three musketeers of Lyon's charcuterie are: the *Rosette*, the *Jésus*, and the *Cervelas*, three various types of sausage.

Jésus, rosette, etc: the whole range of sausages at Targe's.

The 'grattons', a very traditional dish.

'Lyon, Gateway to the South' seems to be the message from this splendid bouillabaisse with Bresse chicken and quenelles, at 'Le Clos des Oliviers' in Croix-Rousse.

The latter is for cooking just like the *Sabodet* which is composed of pork snout and rind.

The *andouillette*, which is a succulent tripe sausage, is considered Lyonnais only if it is mainly composed of crow of veal stuffed in veal skin. Various types of tripes called *gras-double* and *tablier de sapeur* come from a specific part of the veal's stomach called *bonnet de veau*.

Quenelles are also glories of the city's cuisine: these oval-shaped poached delicacies are light, sweet and melt in your mouth. The secret is a balanced proportion of ingredients: pike meat, fat and bread crumbs or semolina.

Lyon has two well-known cheeses: *fromage fort* which means (strong cheese) and the *cervelle de canut* which means (Canut's brain). The first one deserves its name because of the mixture of old cheeses which are marinated in an earthenware pot with white wine and leek stock. The second is made of fromage frais mixed with herbs and shallots.

As for sweets and desserts, Lyon is the proud inventor of *bugne*, a sort of fried doughnut, and *papillottes*, which is a chocolaty sweet.

Lyon's '*third river*', as Léon Daudet called it, is the Beaujolais wine made there. It is still a great success worldwide.

The former capital of the Three Gauls advertises its universally recognised gastronomy, and so it is not surprising that Lyonnais chef Paul Bocuse should have become the worldwide ambassador of French cuisine.

An old favourite invented by the nuns at Saint-Pierre: the 'bugnes'.

Lyon's Murals

Painted walls appear constantly throughout the history of the world, and Lyon is no exception.

In Fourvière, traces of ancient murals can still be among the Roman ruins.

Many churches have preserved what remains of old frescoes on their walls. From 1662 to 1675, Thomas Blanchet, *'painter of Lyon's everyday life'*, decorated the entire town-hall with mythological allegories.

The nineteenth century saw the most productive period for the city's painted walls. The Lyon School of Painting was particularly well-known at the time, notably for its religious works, and benefited from orders boosted by the prosperity of the silk trade. Lyon then became known as the town of the Pre-Raphaelite schools, thanks to artists like Louis Janmot (*Saint-Polycarpe* and *Saint-François-de-Salles* churches) and Hippolyte Flandrin (Saint-Martin-d'Ainay's apse). The stairway of Saint-Pierre's palace is decorated with the portrait of Pierre Puvis de Chavannes, master of Symbolism. In the *Conseil Général* building, Louis-Edouard Fournier painted an immense fresco as a tribute to the Lyon and its Beaujolais wine.

The Cour des Loges mural advertises its Hotel in a very harmonious style. (Mur'Art).

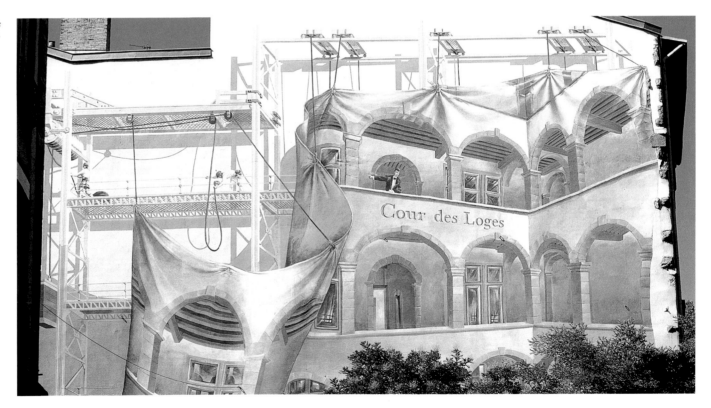

'Le Mur des Canuts' is the most impressive trompe-l'oeil in size and scope in Europe (Cité de la Création).

N° 82 rue Marietton, one of the last murals in the Comics Boulevard by Jacques de Loustal (Mur'Art).

In the twentieth century, three churches were decorated: Saint-Paul's by Paul Borel, Saint-Jacques-le-Majeur's by Louise Cottin and Saint-Pierre-de-Vaise by Claudius Barriot. As far as public edifices went, the ornamentation was impressive. At the Hôtel des Postes, a 55 metre mural painted by Louis Bouquet in 1937 evokes Lyon's themes. In 1934, the façade of the Stock Exchange was decorated by F. Fargeot with an immense mosaic.

Over the last twenty years, more than 150 murals have been designed by painters who wished to promote popular art. This new style of wall-painting, often in the trompe-l'œil style, has been encouraged by public opinion and by organisations like Unesco

On the wall of the Lipha laboratories, 115 avenue Lacassagne, a celebration of Lyon's scientists (Cité de la Création).

View of the Mur des Lyonnais from the Chartreux gardens (Cité de la Création)

which awarded the Tony Garnier Urban Museum a consideration in the '*World Decade in Cultural Development*', in 1991.

Thanks to the teams of painters such as Cité de la Création, Mur'Art and other freelance mural painters, Lyon can be regarded today as the French capital of mural art.

Some of these are exceptional:

The Canut mural, which is the largest trompe-l'œil in Europe with its 1,200 m², commemorates the history of Croix-Rousse Hill (painted by Cité de la Création).

At the foot of the Croix-Rousse Hill, 30 famous characters from the city can be seen on the *Fresque des Lyonnais* (again by Cité de la Création).

In *Vaise*, the *Boulevard de la bande dessinée* (Comics Boulevard), *Rue Marietton* was composed of five painted walls based on the works of contemporary comics artists by Mur'Art. Unfortunately, two have recently been destroyed.

The outstanding *Musée Tony Urbain* exhibits 24 murals on a total surface of 5,500 meters square. They all refer to Tony Garnier's ideal city and the works of six contemporary foreign artists. (Cité de la Création).

The *Porte de la Soie* (door of silk) is part of a project entitled '*Streets of Silk in Lyon's Croix-Rousse*' which was approved by Unesco. It evokes 3,000 years of the city's silk history. (Cité de la Création).

The *Hôtel la Cour des Loges* has acquired a new image with a mural in the shape of a theatre curtain (Mur'Art).

As it runs along the circular route, the enclosing wall of the C.R.I.R. displays the portrait entitled *Marathon de l'Impossible* which holds the likeness of 165 athletes on a 500-metre long mural (Vincent Ducaroy and Mireille Perrin).

Musée Urbain Tony Garnier, detail from a wall by Mexican artist Arturo Guerrero (Cité de la Création).

Quai Saint-Vincent, the library wall. From Rabelais to Clavel, over five centuries, 464 Lyonnais authors (Cité de la Création).

Gates of the Entrance to the Tête d'Or park, built in 1903 by the iron worker Jean Bernard after a design by architect Charles Meysson.

The park's lion, always majestic.

Tropical plants in one of the large greenhouses.

Green Lyon

Lyon is a very green city. Its countryside character is soon apparent as one visits the city. Twenty thousand trees line its streets and another thirty thousand have been counted within its streets and parks. Market gardeners use land within a stone's throw of the *Montée des Soldats* (soldiers' hill).

A new project was launched recently to bring some coherence to this wish for an even greener town. It is essentially based on eliminating sick trees and adding more species of trees and plants to the city's palette, many of which are previously forgotten species. The old plane trees have been replaced with

There are four rose gardens in the park. The oldest one dates from 1930 and is dedicated to show roses; the largest one is situated near the Cité Internationale and dates from 1964. The third is the depositary of roses from historic stock (570 varieties on 1600 m²), and the last one holds wild roses.

Virginian tulip trees, Gingkos, sophoras, limes and Byzantine hazels.

The city's greenness owes much to its parks and squares.

The *Parc de la Tête d'Or* (Golden Head Park) owes its name to the legend that treasure which included a golden Christ's head was buried there. The park was designed by the Bülher brothers in 1856 and covers two hundred and sixty acres, planted with over eight thousand trees. It is considered to be the lungs of the city and many joggers and walkers enjoy its varied paths. It is also famous for its magnificent rose garden in which sixty thousand rosebushes of over three hundred varieties bloom every year. The botanical garden is home to 3,500 species of plants from the entire globe, on its 18 acres and in its 5,000 m² of greenhouse. The zoological gardens shelters 250 mammals, 400 birds and 80 reptiles.

The terraces of *Perrache* are a series of suspended gardens built in 1976, above Perrache's Exchange Center. At the foot of the terraces, one finds the place Carnot, with its statues representing the city of Lyon and the French Republic. One also finds a small curiosity there: in the middle of a flower bed, a milestone covered by a helmet, dating from the Voie Sacrée road of the First World War. It is a reminder of the involvement of Lyon in the Verdun battle, and of the thousands of CBA Berliet trucks which passed by on their way to the frontline.

The gardens of the *Musée des Beaux Arts* are a haven of peace. They were set in the old cloister of the

Place Carnot, a commemorative milestone from the WWI's Voie Sacrée, Verdun – Bar-le-Duc.

The surprising Rosa Mir garden, Croix-Rousse.

Page opposite, the Ceriseraie park's vineyard was traditionally tended by the Canut population. Each plant is sponsored by a personality.

Fourvière's rose pergolas. On the ground are engraved the Rosary's Holy Mysteries.

convent of the Ladies of Saint-Pierre and one can find some moulded samples of the Parthenon friezes as well as mosaics and bronze sculptures by Carpeau, Rodin, Bourdelle, etc.

The Chartreux gardens, which were probably designed by the Bülher brothers in 1855, cover 10.6 hectares. They look like a cascade of terraces flowing down the hill which joins the bank of the Saône with the *Croix-Rousse plateau*. From there, you can get a splendid view of the river and Fourvière Hill.

Place Ampère. On a green background, the eponymous physician sits enthroned.

Following page. Place de la République, where water has replaced trees – a rare occurrence.

At no. *83 Grande Rue* in Croix-Rousse one can find a delightful and discreet little garden, created in the nineteen-fifties by Jules Senis-Mir. This Spanish mason had fled from Franco's regime and slowly created this small Alhambra out of stones and shells, in the memory of his mother, *Rosa Mir*, and the Virgin Mary.

The *jardins de poche*, are small sized gardens which were aimed at creating welcoming green spaces in areas like Croix-Rousse or Vaise, where space is hard to find.

The Rosary Gardens link the basilica to the old town; its southern part is a little paradise where pergolas inspire wonder and meditation.

The fourth biggest park in town is also the least known: *la Ceriseraie* in Croix-Rousse. It has a unique vineyard, whose vines have been individually christened with the names of Lyon's famous people.

In front of the Rédemption church, the Puvis-de-Chavanne square is a veritable fairyland in the Spring, when its fruit trees blossom in pinks and whites around the statue of Joan of Arc.

We shall end this brief list with the Gerland park, which is the youngest of them all, but the third largest with 80 hectares. It is situated next to the Scientific Park, so has taken on a rather didactic character, with its *Maison des Fleurs* whose 350-odd species of plants are cultivated in large beds. Its most popular spot is the skating park, which is open all year long and covers 1,500 m² indoors and 2,400 m² out.

Other green spaces are being planned in many districts. The most impressive will probably be the one on the site of the future *Musée des Confluences*, by the side of its namesake, the confluent of the Saône and the Rhône.

Green is not likely to go out of Lyonnais fashion for a long time for a while yet!

The Rhône and the Saône meet at their confluent, this is the site chosen for the 2005 Science Museum, named 'Cristal-Nuage', like a gigantic space ship amidst fifty hectares of park.

The Maison des Fleurs and its linear plantations, Gerland.

Bibliography

Audin (Amable), *Lyon, miroir de Rome*, Librairie Arthème Fayard, Paris, 1989 ;

Bertin (Dominique) et Clémençon (Anne-Sophie), *Lyon et Villeurbanne*, Guide Arthaud, Paris, 1989 ;

Bouzard (Marie), *La Soierie Lyonnaise du XVIIIe au XXe siècle*, Ed. Lyonnaises d'Art et d'Histoire, Lyon, 1997 ;

Collectif d'auteurs, *Lyon, un site, une cité*, Renaissance du Vieux-Lyon, Lyon, 2000 ;

Corneloup (Gérard), *Les itinéraires du patrimoine mondial*, Office du Tourisme et des Congrès du Grand Lyon, Lyon, 1999 ;

Dejean (René), *Traboules de Lyon, histoire secrète d'une ville*, Editions Le Progrès, Lyon, 1988 ;

Gambier (Gérald), *Les succès de la cuisine Lyonnaise*, Editions La Taillanderie, Châtillon-sur-Chalaronne, 1999 ;

Gambier (Gérald), *Murs peints de Lyon*, Editions La Taillanderie, Châtillon-sur-Chalaronne, 1999 ;

Griffe (Sébastien), *Découvrir Lyon et son patrimoine mondial*, Editions La Taillanderie, Châtillon-sur-Chalaronne, 2000 ;

Jacquemin (Louis), *Histoire des églises de Lyon, Vaulx-en-Velin, Bron, Vénissieux, Saint-Fons*, Ed. Elie Bellier, Lyon, 1985 ;

Jacquemin (Louis), *Lyon, palais et édifices publics*, Editions La Taillanderie, Attignat, 1987 ;

Jacquemin (Louis), *Traboules et Miraboules*, Editions La Taillanderie, Châtillon-sur-Chalaronne, 1999 ;

Mérindol (Pierre), *Lyon, les passerelles du temps*, Editions La Taillanderie, Bourg-en-Bresse, 1988 ;

Neyret (Régis), *Guide historique de Lyon*, Ed du Tricorne, Genève, Ed Lyonnaises d'Art et d'Histoire, Lyon, 1998 ;

Nicolas (Marie-Antoinette), *Le Vieux-Lyon, Old Lyons, 5 circuits*, Edition Lyonnaise d'Art et d'Histoire, Lyon, 1995 ;

Pelletier (André) et Rossiaud (Jacques), *Histoire de Lyon, Antiquité et Moyen Âge*, Ed Horvath, Le Coteau, S.D. ;

Voisin (Dominique), Guillet (Ginette), *La Soie, itinéraires en Rhône-Alpes*, Région Rhône-Alpes, 1989 ;

Wuilleumier (Pierre), *Lyon métropole des Gaules*, Société d'Edition Les Belles Lettres, Paris, 1953.

Le Journal de la Renaissance du Vieux-Lyon ;
Revue Lyon Cité, revue municipale de Lyon ;
La soie, Rhône-Alpes, catalogue ;
Journal Le Progrès.

Achevé d'imprimer en juillet 2006
Dépôt légal 3e trimestre 2006
Printed in China